The Lost Art of Ironing

First published 2024 by The Hedgehog Poetry Press,

5 Coppack House, Churchill Avenue, Clevedon. BS21 6QW

www.hedgehogpress.co.uk

ISBN: 978-1-916830-30-1

Cover image credit:

Edgar Degas, *Woman Ironing,* begun c. 1876, completed c. 1887, oil on canvas
Collection of Mr and Mrs Paul Mellon, 1972.74.1, Not on view
Courtesy National Gallery of Art, Washington

Author photo credit:

Kelly Davis at Maryport Harbour © Clare Park, www.clarepark.com

The Lost Art of Ironing

by

Kelly Davis

Contents

For Ian

TO MY HANDS

When I slid into the world,
you came out clenched, like two walnuts,
then you gradually uncurled, finding your way
into mouths, eyes, porridge.

Later you wrapped yourselves round stubby pencils
to form my first As, Bs and Cs.
A few years on, I gnawed your nails
in my worried teenage mouth,
your fingers made discoveries
in the slick coral heart of me.

Soon you moved fast enough
to make boys spill their seed.
You balanced cigarettes, held soggy joints,
trailed in rivers beside lazy boats,
fanned out like angelfish
as I swam in the South China Sea.

You wielded an editor's blue pen:
insert, rewrite, delete, stet.
Later still, you learned to type
on an Amstrad's qwerty keyboard,
sent faxes, never mastered texts,
graduated to desktops, laptops.

In between, you rubbed off cradle cap,
tested milk – too hot or just right,
wiped babies' bottoms, smeared on cream,
combed thistledown hair, snapped poppers,
did minimal washing and ironing,
waved tall sons off to university.

You are still labouring,
pecking away on keyboards –
more stiffly now.
Your veins form a relief map.
Your papery skin has lines
that gather on your finger joints.

At night I often wake
to find you tightly clenched.

IF EMILY DICKINSON WERE MY BEST FRIEND

I'd visit her in Amherst,
climb the wooden stair
and knock gently
on her bedroom door.

I'd ask her to tell me her secret,
how to distil 200 words into 20,
how to capture a truth
before it slipped away –

I'd tell her the sun was shining,
book two tickets to Paris,
take her to the Musée Rodin,
suggest she unpin her hair.

We'd go to a bar in Montparnasse,
drink gin and tonic from big glasses,
talk about how women's lives
had changed – and not changed.

I'd try to take away her sadness
even though her sadness made me love her.
I'd ask if she knew she'd become an icon,
if that was what she wanted?

Then I'd take her back to her room,
make sure she had all she needed:
a jug of water, a Bible, notebook and pen,
a choice about how to live, and when.

AN ENIGMA RESOLVED

If I stare at you hard enough,
perhaps I can time-travel
through a wormhole
back to a day in 1504
when sitting for your portrait
was no longer a novelty.

Your weekly visits
had continued for more than a year
and you'd grown to loathe the smell of paint.
You settled yourself in a wooden chair,
tucked a faded velvet cushion
behind the small of your back

sighed and arranged your hands
the way he liked them,
right over left.
At first you tried making conversation
but he seemed more interested
in the skulls on his shelves.

So you emptied your mind,
sank into soporific silence,
waited for the hours to slide away.
The weight of centuries
pressed down on you,
squeezed the air from your lungs.

No sound but the clock
and Leonardo's slipper'd feet
shuffling back and forth.
Nothing of interest at all
until you saw, on the wall,
a fly struggling in a web   and almost smiled.

VALLDEMOSSA

In 1838 Frédéric Chopin made an ill-fated trip to Mallorca with the novelist George Sand,
known to friends as Aurore, accompanied by her two children.

The sighing wind,
the drumming rain,
his hacking cough,
her scratching pen,
children's voices in stone corridors:
Maurice! Solange!　　　*Maman!*

The love and pain
he poured into
the notes he wrote,
the melodies
that trickled through
his fingers　　onto the keys.

Beginning with single chimes,
then deeper, darker chords,
massing storm clouds,
raindrops quickening,
like the pulse in his head
until at last　　the music ended.

In the trembling light of day,
drops glistened on leaves.
Frédéric and Aurore,
exhausted, sipped bitter coffee,
picked at stale breakfast pastries,
wished it could be　　as it was before.

I SAT OPPOSITE AUTUMN ON THE TUBE

After John Keats

I sat opposite Autumn on the Tube,
I think it was the Circle Line.
She wouldn't meet my eye,
just sat there tight-lipped,
reading her book.

I noticed a slight *fume of poppies*
from a sad-looking addict
lying on a dirty sleeping bag
as I followed Autumn through a tunnel
to the Northern Line.

Her hair was mostly under a woolly hat
but as we stood on the platform
a few wisps were *soft lifted*
by the winnowing wind
when the next train whooshed in.

I admit she had a *patient look*
as we rattled all the way
to Morden. Leaving the station
in the *soft-dying day*, I batted away
a cloud of whining gnats.

But there were no lambs,
hedge-crickets, robins
or swallows to be seen.
And then Autumn disappeared
down a side street.

SELF-PORTRAIT, PARIS, 1915

After T.S. Eliot

He came again this evening – for *apéritifs*.
I couldn't resist arranging the room and myself
to our best advantage:
lilacs in a bowl, curtains drawn against the dusk.
I wore my mauve silk, with my hair up.

In the soft candlelight, I hoped
my skin would look unlined.

When we first met
I thought there was a spark.
We laughed, drank champagne,
talked of Chopin and poetry,
met in the park.

Tonight my heart almost fluttered
when I heard his step on the stair,
his diffident knock at the door.
But he came in looking pale,
distracted, sat in silence.

I talked of this and that,
until I bored myself as well as him.

I ended the evening brightly,
assured him I would continue
to enjoy my life in Paris.
After all, I have so many friends,
so many ways to pass the time.

THE CHANGE

Lying like a starfish on a sweaty bed,
toes reaching desperately for a patch of cool sheet,
it comes to me that the long-awaited change
is finally occurring.

It's actually been sneaking up for quite a while:
that sense of brittleness,
the unfamiliar aches and pains,
the last-gasp sexual appetite.

Maybe this is why so many women go slightly mad:
have drastic plastic surgery, take young lovers.
Nature urges us to spend the last sweetness of our bodies
when the world just wishes we would go quietly.

THE LOST ART OF IRONING

I usually fold things straight from the tumble-dryer
but yesterday I left some napkins in too long and they came out
scrunched as old tissues.

Nothing for it but to resurrect the dusty iron.
And I felt almost joyful, pressing down on the hot metal,
transforming crumpled cloth into neat squares.

I thought of all the women before me,
ironing each day, smoothing out life's creases,
creating order from heaps of chaos.

My mother-in-law lived through the war
and ironed everything – dishcloths, towels, underpants,
every bit of fabric in the house.

She couldn't talk about her feelings
but she ironed beautifully. Her children knew she loved them
because their sheets were always smooth as glass.

GOOGLING DEAD FRIENDS

There may be a Facebook page
with posts that stop abruptly,
followed by emotional tributes, crying emojis
or – weirdly – messages to the deceased
as if they could still reply.

And there's the usual Internet trail –
left-over professional listings,
media mentions, maybe some photos,
and the odd surprise,
like that book you never knew they'd written.

People used to burn letters
they wanted no one to read,
destroy evidence
of illicit loves, shameful deeds.
Now it all stays in the Cloud forever and ever, amen.

And random sins are left floating
in the digital ocean, like pale body parts,
to be netted by ghoulish voyeurs.
Time was, you could edit your own legacy
but now the monstrous truth will out.

PROVE YOUR IDENTITY

Enter: Personal possession
A filigree necklace, once taken
from Edwardian England to a farm
in the Orange Free State:
talisman of transit and survival.

Enter: Location
Cumbria for more than half my life:
North London Jewish girl adrift,
interloper, blow-in, link in diaspora chain,
drop in an ocean of DNA rain.

Enter: Mother's maiden name
Weitzman.
Her father left Lithuania in time.

MY GREAT-GRANDMOTHER'S NECKLACE

It's always been with me.
Draped on a dressing table,
glinting above a neckline,
its filigree spirals and turquoise beads
sparking compliments from strangers.

Katie wore it in London as a young girl
and in the Orange Free State as a matriarch.
She left her life in the bustling city,
endured that voyage with boxes and trunks –
the necklace coiled in a silken pouch.

In Vrede, she and her new husband
made their home in a hut with a dirt floor.
The necklace survived those dusty days –
memento of Edwardian England,
fringe of finely worked metallic lace.

I've been a careless custodian.
Once it disappeared for weeks
but I knew it would return.
When I opened the washing machine, there it was –
a tiny silver snake nestled in the rubber seal.

TRYING TO EDIT THE HOLOCAUST

I delete a word here,
smooth a phrase there,
remove repetition, modify the tone.

The material is too raw.
We must present it in a form
that can be easily digested.

The pictures must be carefully selected,
not too gruesome. Our readers
mustn't turn away.

Even the truth must be packaged.
It's paid work that should
be done professionally.

Yet every now and then
I hear echoes of another story:
the one my mother told me.

The day her Lithuanian father
opened a letter that made him bellow
like a wounded bull.

The day he heard
that his parents, brothers, brothers' wives
and children had all been shot.

That story also
had photos of dark-eyed relatives
left behind.

He planned to earn enough to bring them all to Africa.
But history caught them, and their bodies fell
into the pit.

Under the pile of corpses lay his friend.
When night fell, he fled, then sent a letter,
via the Red Cross, to a Durban address.

Years later, after the war,
Grandpa's friend returned to reclaim his house,
and was murdered by his ex-neighbours.

No uplifting end to that story,
just a final deletion.
Yet – here we still are.

ON READING ANNE SEXTON

I started reading your words
and couldn't stop.
Everything seemed pointless
beside your maggoty mind
in all its raging glory.

You could not see the sea
without imagining its cold embrace.
You lacked a carapace.
You turned to the world womb-side out,
defied your fate – and leapt towards it.

RISK ASSESSMENT

Walking along the prom
I make a judgement about the waves.
Are they licking the edge of the path
or swallowing it whole?

Will my dog and I be safe
beside this body of water
that is sometimes calm and still,
sometimes shuddering, convulsing?

Next to the path are signs of past storms:
concrete blocks pulverised into fragments,
bits of metal and plastic
vomited onto the shore.

Above me, the steep slope
has become a cliff,
chunks of earth
bitten out.

We used to build sandcastles on holiday.
We'd make the walls higher, the moats deeper,
then watch, helpless,
as our castles vanished.

WHITE GLADIOLI

I thought of you today
although it happened years ago.
I saw the tattered flowers
marooned amongst the bracken,
their stems bent over.
Riding your bike that summer,
you went somewhere you never meant to go.
When your tea got cold
your mum must have wondered where you were.
She probably clicked her tongue.
The gladioli are there,
where your bike bore you over the edge.
I see you in mid-air –
wheels spinning like a cartoon –
dropping into nothingness.

Dropping into nothingness –
wheels spinning like a cartoon –
I see you in mid-air,
where your bike bore you over the edge.
The gladioli are there.
She probably clicked her tongue.
Your mum must have wondered where you were
when your tea got cold.
You went somewhere you never meant to go,
riding your bike that summer.
Their stems bent over,
marooned amongst the bracken,
I saw the tattered flowers.
Although it happened years ago,
I thought of you today.

EDITING MEMOIRS

Sometimes I feel like Florence Nightingale
wandering the battlefield at night,
hearing dying men calling for their mothers,
wishing I could reattach their severed limbs,
return the blood to their veins.

Looking back, perhaps it was a mistake to say
I specialised in memoirs. I never thought
so many wounded lives would fling themselves
into my in-box, beg me to heal them,
arrange them neatly on the page.

WALKING IN APRIL

Chilly Spring slides sideways into Summer.
On the farm track, hacked-back
hedgerows overlook grassy banks
of burnished buttercups
and gleaming golden gorse.
How quickly rain-soaked soil
can dry into parched powder.
Some fields striped with tractor tyre-marks,
torn trenches and topsoil ridges;
others, raked smooth as seed-trays,
surveyed by blackbirds who busily
wrench up wriggling worms.
High above, a solitary seagull glides
on a secret mission across blue skies.

SENHOUSE STREET, MARYPORT

If this street were a woman
she'd be stubbing out her fag
remembering better days.

A few pubs hang off her sleeves
along with the charity shops.

A newsagent and the last bank
linger, like stray hairpins.

The pavement's a paisley skirt
of nameless stains.

At dusk, youths drift
near the chip shop, the alleyway,
smoking and swearing

while gulls watch for pickings
from chimney battlements.

She could be a street
in any left-behind northern town
but she has a giddy secret.

Over the brow of the hill,
she careers down to a harbour,
a once-grand quay

swirls of green nets,
a host of masts,
the *best* bloody sunsets in England.

THE BIG ROOM

This is the room that made us buy the house,
with its moss-green velvet curtains opening
on a perfect view across the Solway Firth –
Scottish mountains rising out of swirling, inky mist,
subtle as a Japanese silk painting.
On crisp, blue-sky days, the windows frame
an Ordnance Survey map of fields.
On summer evenings, blood-orange sunsets
paint rhomboids on the walls.

When we arrived, I was pregnant with my second son
and later sat in the worn leather club chair to feed him.
Every Christmas, we opened presents
by the glowing fire, piled on logs
till flames leapt up the chimney.
During power cuts, we huddled round the embers,
played Scrabble by candlelight.
Once a bird flapped down
and burst out, sooty and terrified.

In the 1880s, Alfred Hine, joint owner
of the Holme Shipping Line,
man of taste and learning,
lived here with family and servants.
When Oscar Wilde visited Maryport
to lecture on 'The Value of Art',
he may have leant a velvet-clad elbow
on this marble mantelpiece, gazed up
at the piped-cream mouldings on the ceiling.

Guests' mouths have gaped
at the sight of this room.
With furniture pushed back,
it's big enough for dancing.
The walls have shaken to Irish jigs
played on fiddle, banjo and flute.
But now it's mostly just the two of us
reading quietly in armchairs
on either side of the hearth.

When we leave, new caretakers will move in
with packing cases and toddlers.
May this door open wide for them
as it did for us.

SYCAMORES

Your branches curve
over the gravel drive
like a mother's arms.
Sometimes your brittle fingers snap
and lie scattered below,
offered up as kindling.

We should have booked a tree surgeon years ago
to trim and prune and make you safe,
but we've left you to your own devices.

You and the wind
whisper secrets,
singing mournfully together,
squabbling and moaning,
needing each other
as the earth needs the rain.

THE ARCHED WINDOW IN MY SON'S BEDROOM

So near the floor it's almost a door –
to blue sky, another dimension.

When he was a toddler it gave me nightmares –
that awful story of Eric Clapton's son falling to his death.

We kept it locked so long we lost the key –
the wide sill a harmless perch for a schoolboy.

He could look down on trees that resembled bushes
while seagulls flew past at pale-yellow eye level.

When we had scaffolding, he picked the lock and sunbathed
on the boards, assured me it was safe.

During lockdown, his quiet room became
the perfect study, with window as relief.

Now he's left, the arched glass offers
a vertiginous view for passing guests.

They meet the seagulls, eyeball to eyeball,
each in their element.

LENTIL SOUP

When I think of us
I think of lentil soup:
its belly-filling warmth
the crusty bread we dip.

I think of the gorgeous traces
it leaves on our hob:
the scattered orange sequins
the tiny frills of parsley lace
the curlicues of dried oil
the salt sprinkled like glitter.

When I think of us
I think of lentil soup:
the way there's always more,
the way it costs as little
and as much
as love.

MAKE THE TIME

After Seamus Heaney

Make the time
to let your mind wander
where it will. Resist the urge
to keep working or scrolling
on your phone.
Allow your thoughts to unfold
like magnolia buds, beginning tightly closed,
ending as huge, pale pink goblets,
drinking in the sights, sounds, smells.
And in that same moment,
make the time
to let the closed book of your heart
fall open – so you can read
the poems pulsing through it.

CUTTING THROUGH THE FIELDS

Today I surprised you
by recognising a yellowhammer's call
and you pointed out a brambling, balanced on a bramble.
He was brownish, with a white collar and a rosy chest –
and there was a female facing him, a few feet away.

Then we saw some sandstone slabs on the shore
with ripple patterns, which you said
had nothing to do with the sea
and everything to do with events
that occurred millions of years ago.

And on the way back
we cut through the fields –
and brushed our hands
through the feathery barley stalks
as if we were five years old.

MEETING IN DEEP TIME

I'm on a journey inside my husband's head. We normally exist in different worlds – me with my words, him with his rocks. But now I'm editing his book and travelling back 400 million years. I'm starting to understand how slowly tectonic plates meet and move apart; how layers of rock can shift; how they thrust, fold, edge into one another's space; how vast glaciers freeze the warm earth and thaw into torrents, sculpting jagged peaks and scooping out deep valleys. I'm seeing orange pyroclastic flows obliterate ancient slopes; and swarms of rounded drumlins under the grass, like whales breaking the surface; realising that a million years is the tiniest sliver of time; that the two of us, and every thought we've ever had, are at once utterly unimportant and infinitely precious.

AFTER SONNET 1: FROM FAIREST CREATURES WE DESIRE INCREASE

If all the supermodels on the earth
could clone themselves, they'd live for evermore.
But artificial youth has little worth
and beauty set in stone becomes a bore.
In days gone by, the choice was very stark:
you had your children young or not at all.
But now the test tubes wait in freezers dark
and no one hears their silent, plaintive call.
The surgeon's knife preserves the teenage grin,
celebrity provides its own reward,
time's ravages are hidden by smooth skin,
self-love is now our cult, our god, our lord.
If age no longer takes a much-loved face,
has time been conquered by the human race?

AFTER SONNET 2: WHEN FORTY WINTERS SHALL BESIEGE THY BROW

When forty years have passed and done their worst
and lines appear upon your forehead fair,
your peachy skin that now looks fit to burst
will bunch and sag like clothes too big to wear.
That faddy diet will leave you skin and bone,
your blood will slow and gradually grow cold.
You may then ask where all your beauty's flown.
What happened to the pin-up looks of old?
A pile of selfies may be all that's left.
Not much, it seems, for all there is to show
of life – with all its twists, its warp and weft.
Nothing is reaped by those who never sow.
To bear a child might well have kept you young,
a ball of life towards the future flung.

AFTER SONNET 18: SHALL I COMPARE THEE TO A SUMMER'S DAY?

Are you like a sunny holiday snap?
No – you're more of a poignant, fleeting shot.
We miss the perfect picture when we nap.
One moment summer's here, and then it's not.
The sun so often burns too hot and bright
and must be filtered to avoid a glare.
We all have photos we keep out of sight,
the ones we hide from the stranger's cold stare.
But your Instagrammed beauty will not die,
your virtual lips will keep their cherry red.
On Facebook we can't tell truth from a lie,
or vibrant, young and fair from nearly dead.
So long as screens still glow and pixels shine,
your image will live on, defying time.

AFTER SONNET 27: WEARY WITH TOIL, I HASTE ME TO MY BED

There is no rest in darkness black and deep
when Google stalkers sit up through the night.
A well-lit screen can make a grown man weep
until his eyes are red, his chest is tight.
No pill can numb the endless, nagging ache
of unacknowledged, unrequited lust.
With hands like claws, he suffers for her sake,
and types her name once more – because he must.
Meanwhile, oblivious, she leads her life,
awakes, logs on and enters cyberspace.
Her every post then stabs him like a knife,
his mind is filled with screenshots of her face.
What doesn't kill him worsens the disease,
turns dreams to nightmares, brings him to his knees.

AFTER SONNET 73: THAT TIME OF YEAR THOU MAY'ST IN ME BEHOLD

Don't write me any love songs for the young
for what they know of life is sparse at best.
On waves of Tinder passion they are flung,
they swipe and click - and seldom pass time's test.
But those of us whose hair is touched with grey,
who know the words of those autumnal blues,
prefer the gentle twilight to the day
and trade the sudden blaze for the slow fuse.
So knowledge is denied to careless youth.
With age we gain the wisdom that we need,
yet also learn a melancholy truth:
we are consumed by that on which we feed.
At last we know that love is what life's for,
and life is short - so *we* love even more.

ACKNOWLEDGEMENTS

My deepest thanks to the editors who first selected these poems.

To My Hands: *Aesthetica Creative Writing Award* Anthology, 2021; also commended by Alison Brackenbury in the Fire River Poets Competition, 2016

If Emily Dickinson were My Best Friend, Valldemossa, Lentil Soup: *Erbacce Poetry Journal*, Issue 69, 2022

An Enigma Resolved: *Reflected Light: Responses to the Creative Arts*, Grey Hen Press, 2020

I Sat Opposite Autumn on the Tube: *London Grip*, Spring 2023

The Lost Art of Ironing: This work was originally published in *Mslexia* magazine (Issue 100, December 2023), www.mslexia.co.uk

The Change: *Glory Days*, Hen Run, Grey Hen Press, 2021

White Gladioli: This work was originally published in *Mslexia* magazine (Issue 76, December 2018), www.mslexia.co.uk

On Reading Anne Sexton: *Quirk*, Issue 7, 2016

Trying to Edit the Holocaust: *The Journal*, Issue 55, 2017

Prove Your Identity: First prize, Magma Subscribers' Competition, 2018; also published in *Two Ravens: Explorations of mind and memory*, Grey Hen Press, 2024

Meeting in Deep Time: *Magma Poetry,* Issue 81, Anthropocene

After Sonnet 2: When Forty Winters Shall Besiege Thy Brow: *Poetry for Performance*, The Playing Space, 2017

After Sonnet 18: Shall I Compare Thee to a Summer's Day? Third prize, Poetry Charm Competition, judged by Polly Walshe, 2022

I am also very grateful to my fellow poets at North Cumbria Stanza and Northwest Poets for their invaluable feedback; to all those at the Carlisle Speakeasy and Poets Out Loud open mics; to poetry mentors Kim Moore and Angela Locke, who inspired me to write several of these poems; and – above all – to Mark Davidson, at Hedgehog Poetry Press, for publishing my first solo collection.